Young Rider's

GUIDE TO

Riding a Horse
or Pony

Young Rider's

GUIDE TO

Riding a Horse or Pony

LESLEY WARD

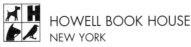

HOWELL BOOK HOUSE
NEW YORK

This book is not intended as a substitute for professional advice and guidance. A young person should take part in the activities discussed in this book only under the supervision of a knowledgeable adult.

Howell Book House
A Simon & Schuster Macmillan Company
1633 Broadway
New York, NY 10019

MACMILLAN is a registered trademark of Macmillan, Inc.

Library of Congress Cataloging-in-Publication Data

Ward, Lesley.
    Young rider's guide to riding a horse or pony / Lesley Ward.
    p. cm.
    ISBN 0-87605-928-0
    1. Horsemanship—Juvenile literature. 2. Ponies—Juvenile literature.
    [1. Horsemanship. 2. Horses. 3. Ponies.] I. Title.
SF309.2.W37 1996
798.2'3—dc20   96-2846
                                                                  CIP
                                                                  AC

Manufactured in the United States of America

10 9 8 7 6 5 4 3 2 1

BOOK DESIGN BY GEORGE J. MCKEON

Contents

Introduction

If you are like most horse people, you probably think riding is the best sport in the world. But how good a rider are you? Do you bounce around like a sack of potatoes, or do you sit quietly and securely on your horse?

If you really want to be a good rider, you must be willing to take lessons and spend lots of time in the saddle. It is also very important that you find a friendly instructor who will help you improve your riding skills. Even top riders have coaches!

Becoming a good rider won't happen overnight. It takes hard work and practice. If you are just starting out, this book will teach you the basics that you need. It will help you to develop an excellent riding position and teach you how to ride a horse at any speed.

You'll also learn all about fun activities like jumping and trail riding. So start reading. After you've finished this book, you may be the best rider at the barn!

1 Getting Started

If you are serious about riding, one of the most important things you must do is find a good riding instructor and sign up for regular lessons. If you don't have your own horse, you can go to a riding school.

CHOOSING A RIDING SCHOOL

Look in the yellow pages of your telephone book to see if there are any riding schools near you. One or two may be advertised, but it is difficult to tell from an ad if a school is good or not.

If you have a friend who rides at a school already, ask her what she thinks of it. If she likes the school, your parents can call the manager and ask to look around while lessons are going on. When you visit, keep the following points in mind.

First Impressions

The riding school employees should be friendly, and someone should be happy to give you a quick tour. The employees should be dressed in appropriate clothing like jodhpurs or jeans and boots—not shorts and sandals!

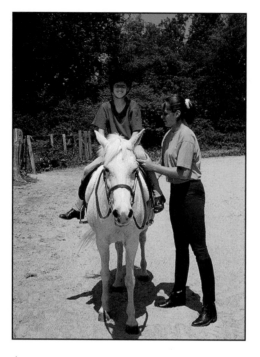

A RIDING SCHOOL SHOULD HAVE FRIENDLY HELPERS.

THE BARN MUST BE NEAT AND TIDY.

An important question is whether the teachers are experienced. At least one person on the staff should have taught for many years or gone to a college with a riding program.

The Barn

The stable area should be tidy. Manure and straw should be swept onto a muck heap, and the stables should be clean. If horses are standing in piles of manure or puddles, it's best to leave and find another school!

The buildings must be in good repair. There should not be any broken glass or equipment with sharp edges that could hurt you or a horse. People should not smoke! One spark can set a bale of hay alight and cause a fire.

The Horses and Ponies

The animals should look alert and interested in what is going on around them. They must also be well groomed and look like they have enough to eat. You shouldn't be able to see their ribs sticking out.

Don't ride at a school where the horses look tired and in poor condition. Ask how many times a day a horse is ridden. The horses should be used in no more than three lessons per day. You don't want to ride a tired horse that has been ridden five times in a row.

Employees should be kind and firm. They should not shout at horses or beat them.

The Lessons

Watch a lesson and pay close attention. Does the school match students with horses by size and ability? If you are small, you don't want to ride a huge horse. A pony would suit you better. If you have never ridden before, you don't want to ride a mean horse or one that is frisky. That's no fun!

Do all the students wear safety helmets? Even the safest horse can spook or stumble, causing his rider to take a fall.

There should be no more than six students to a lesson. If there are more, the teacher can't spend enough time with you

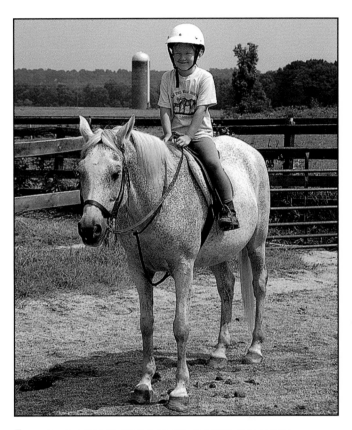

THIS RIDING SCHOOL HORSE LOOKS HEALTHY AND HAPPY.

THERE SHOULD BE NO MORE THAN SIX STUDENTS IN A LESSON.

individually. A good teacher encourages her students and doesn't yell at them.

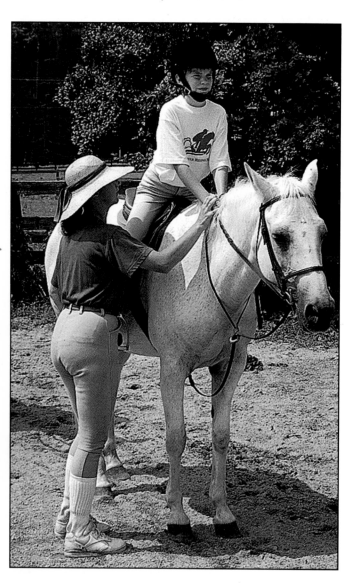

A GOOD TEACHER WILL SPEND TIME WITH YOU.

WHAT YOU SHOULD WEAR TO RIDE

Don't buy expensive riding clothes right away. A pair of jeans and low-heeled shoes with laces or boots are fine for your first lessons. Don't wear sneakers, because you need heels to keep your feet in the stirrups.

One way to save money on riding clothes is by checking your riding school's bulletin board. An older student may sell jodhpurs or boots he or she has outgrown.

Let's take a look at basic riding gear that you will need if you are going to ride regularly.

A Riding Helmet

A helmet is the most important item of safety gear you can own. You should never ride without one! If you are going to continue taking lessons, ask your parents to buy you an ASTM/SEI-approved safety riding helmet. This helmet meets the tough standards set by the American Society for Testing and Materials (ASTM) and has the Safety Equipment Institute (SEI) seal. Buy it at a tack shop and have it properly fitted. Don't buy a used helmet because you may not be able to tell just by looking at it if it has been dented or damaged.

There are several types of helmets. Velvet hats with peaks are used in the showring because they look elegant.

Jockey skull caps are used by jockeys and eventers (people who ride cross-country and jump big fences), but they are suitable for young riders, too. Most riders cover a skull cap with a colorful hat cover.

Schooling helmets are like lightweight bicycle helmets. You can put a velvet cover on them for formal occasions.

If your school supplies you with a helmet, make sure it fits properly. If it is too loose or too tight, it won't protect you if you fall off your horse. A helmet must have a permanent chin strap and you must use it.

Have your instructor help you test the helmet's size. Put the hat on and lean over. If your instructor can wiggle the helmet around, it is too big.

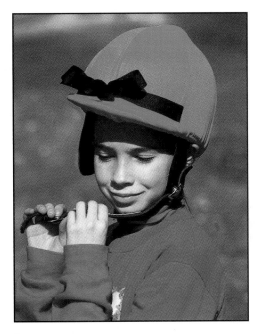

PUT A COLORFUL COVER ON YOUR HELMET.

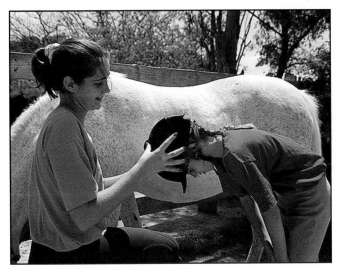

IF A HAT WIGGLES, DON'T WEAR IT.

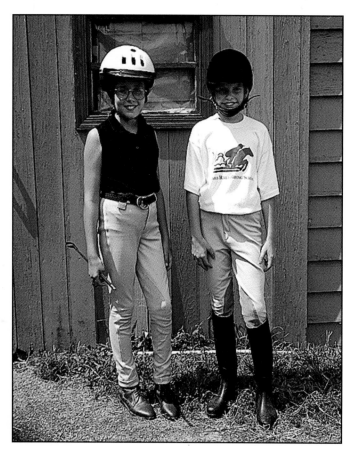

Two well-dressed riders.

Jodhpurs and Breeches

Jeans or trousers are fine for riding lessons. If you can afford them, buy jodhpurs. They are more comfortable and won't rub your legs like jeans.

Jodhpurs go down to your feet. You wear them with short boots.

Breeches are shorter and are worn with tall boots.

Jodhpurs and breeches come in many colors. If you can only afford one pair, buy beige because you can wear them in shows.

Footwear

Your riding footwear should have low heels. Otherwise your feet will slip out of the stirrups, which is dangerous.

If you are new to riding, buying inexpensive tall rubber boots is a good idea. When they get dirty you can wash them off, and you can polish them to look nice for a show. Tall leather boots can wait until you start to compete regularly.

You can also wear short paddock boots. They are ankle high and have laces.

Chaps

Chaps are leather leggings that are worn over jodhpurs, jeans, or even shorts (in the summer). They fasten with zippers on the sides. Chaps must fit snugly or they

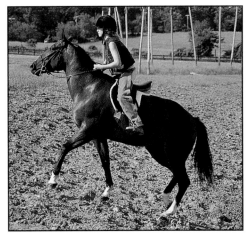

CHAPS CAN EVEN BE WORN OVER SHORTS.

THESE CLOTH GLOVES HAVE RUBBER GRIPS.

may rub your legs and make them sore. Chaps are for casual riding only. You can't wear chaps at a show.

Gloves

Wearing gloves when you ride is a smart idea. They protect your hands from blisters and give you a firm grip on the reins in wet weather. They also keep your hands warm in winter.

You don't need fancy leather gloves. An inexpensive pair of cloth gloves with rubber grips is fine.

2 In the Saddle

The first time you ride a horse can be a bit scary. But if you have a good instructor to help you, you should be fine. You'll be riding in no time at all.

FIT AS A FIDDLE

You need to be fit and flexible if you are going to ride. You won't become a good rider if you huff and puff after two minutes of trotting! Regular exercise makes you a better rider. Stay in shape by swimming or riding your bike. Do a few jumping jacks or situps every day. Mucking out a stable is good exercise, too!

LEADING A HORSE

Before you hop on your horse, you will probably lead him to a ring. Lift both reins over his head and hold on to them with your right hand, about three inches below his chin. Hold the excess reins with your left hand. Never let the reins drag on the ground, because your horse could step on them and break them. Tack is expensive, so treat it with care!

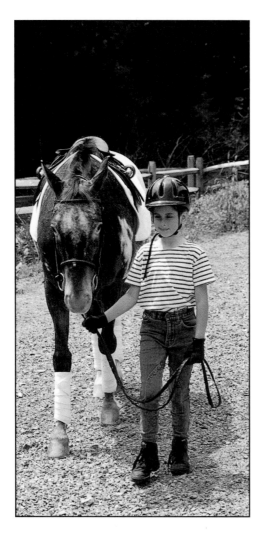

HOLD THE REINS WITH BOTH HANDS WHEN LEADING.

Face forward, stand next to your horse's shoulder, and tell him to "Walk on" when you move forward. When you want to stop, give a small tug on the reins with your right hand, say "Whoa," and stop. If your horse doesn't halt, give one or two gentle tugs on the reins.

MOUNTING A HORSE

Some people grab the saddle and pull themselves up inch by inch, but mounting this way can hurt the horse and damage the saddle, too! Here is the best way to mount a horse:

1. Make sure your stirrups are the right length. An easy way to tell is to run your stirrups down, hold your right arm straight out in front of you, and touch the saddle with your knuckles. Then lift the stirrup iron with your left hand and hold it under your right arm. The iron should hit you at your right armpit.

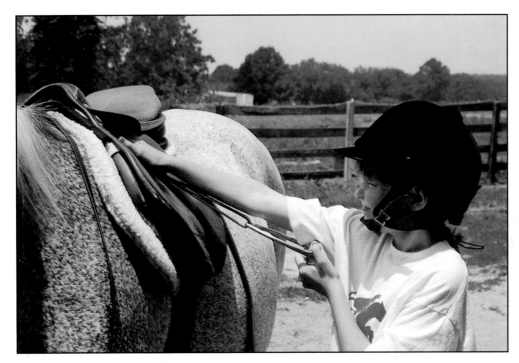

CHECK THE
LENGTH OF
YOUR STIRRUPS.

Then check the girth to make sure it is tight. If it is loose the saddle will move when you try to mount and it could end up under your horse's belly.

2. Stand at your horse's left shoulder, facing his tail.

3. Hold the reins with your left hand and the stirrup iron with your right. Slip your left foot in the stirrup.

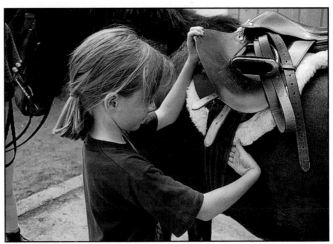

MAKE SURE THE GIRTH ISN'T LOOSE.

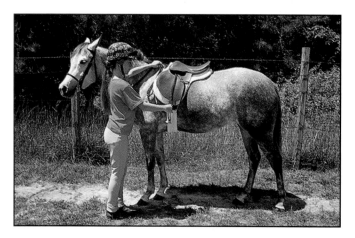

A. FACE YOUR HORSE'S TAIL.

B. PUT YOUR LEFT FOOT IN THE STIRRUP.

C. HOP AROUND ON YOUR RIGHT FOOT.

D. LEAP UP INTO THE AIR.

4. Grab some of the horse's mane with your left hand. Rest your right hand on the saddle's pommel (front) or on the seat. Then bounce around on your right foot until you are facing forward. Be careful you don't kick your horse in the ribs. Give three big bounces and hop lightly into the air.

5. Slowly raise your right leg over your horse's back. Try not to bang your leg on his backside.

6. Gently lower yourself into the saddle. Never slam down on your horse's back. This hurts him. Next, put your right foot in the stirrup. If you have safety stirrups, make sure the rubber band is on the outside.

SWING YOUR RIGHT LEG OVER THE HORSE'S BACK.

SIT DOWN GENTLY.

13

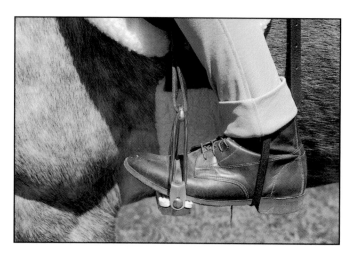

THE RUBBER BAND ON A SAFETY STIRRUP GOES ON THE OUTSIDE.

MOUNTING BLOCK

Sometimes you may need help mounting a horse. He may be too big for you to hop on by yourself, or he may have a sensitive back and must be mounted gently. This is when you use a mounting block. Walk the horse next to the block, ask him to halt, and climb aboard.

A LEG UP!

A pony pal can help you mount by giving you a "leg up." Here's how it's done:

1. Stand facing the horse and lift your left leg up. Your friend holds your lower left leg, below the knee, with both hands.

2. Bounce three times on your right leg (count with your friend) and on the third

BRING YOUR HORSE CLOSE TO THE MOUNTING BLOCK. THEN SWING YOUR RIGHT LEG OVER HIS BACK.

HAVE A PAL GRAB YOUR LEFT LEG, THEN
BOUNCE THREE TIMES.

bounce, your friend lifts you
up in the air.

3. Swing your right leg over the
horse's back and lower yourself
gently into the saddle. Be careful that your friend doesn't lift

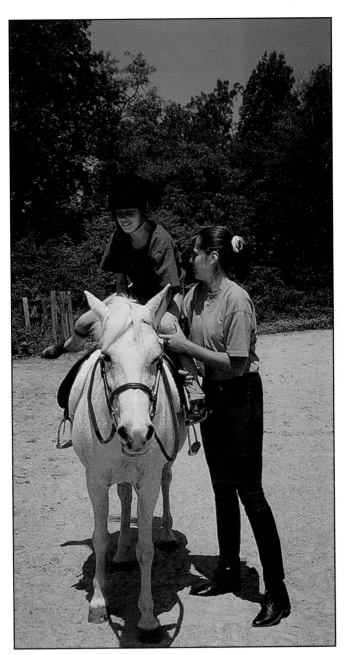

SIT DOWN QUIETLY.

15

you too high or you might fly over the horse and end up on the ground! Practice on a quiet horse.

ADJUSTING YOUR STIRRUPS

Once you are in the saddle, check that your stirrups are the correct length. Take your feet out of the stirrups and hang your legs down. Your ankles should be next to the bottom of the stirrup.

If the stirrups are too long or too short, adjust them without dismounting. Keep your foot in the

STIRRUPS SHOULD HIT YOU AT THE ANKLE.

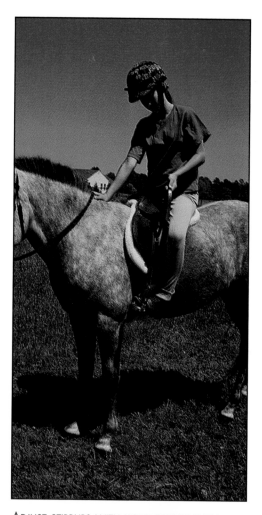

ADJUST STIRRUPS WITH YOUR FEET IN THEM.

stirrup and lift your leg in front of the saddle so you can get to the buckle underneath the flap.

CHECK THAT GIRTH!

Before you get going, check the girth. Some horses suck air into their bellies when you tighten the girth the first time. Then they let the air out after you mount. The girth loosens and—whoops! The next thing you know, the saddle slips and you are on the ground.

Hold your left leg up and lift the saddle flap to check if the girth needs to go up a hole or two.

DISMOUNTING

Hopping off a horse is easy. Just follow these steps:

1. Take both feet out of the stirrups. Hold both reins in your

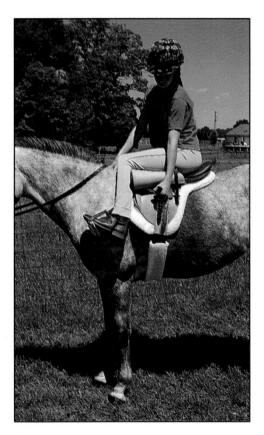

CHECK THE GIRTH BEFORE YOU MOVE.

TAKE YOUR FEET OUT OF THE STIRRUPS WHEN READY TO DISMOUNT.

17

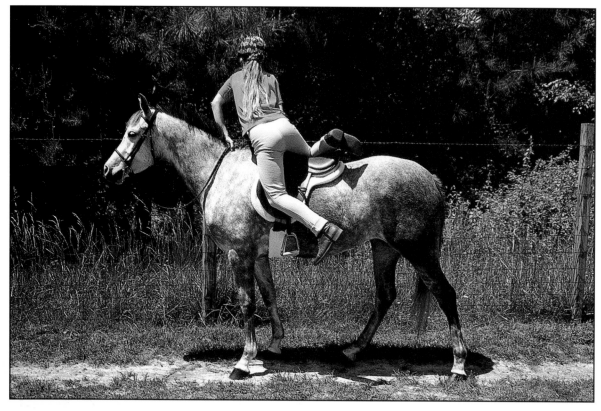

SWING YOUR RIGHT LEG OVER YOUR HORSE'S BACK.

PUT YOUR LEGS TOGETHER AND SLIDE DOWN.

left hand. Rest your right hand on the saddle or on your horse's withers.

2. Gently swing your right leg over your horse's back.

3. Put both your legs together and bend at the knees as you head for the ground. Bending helps soften your landing.

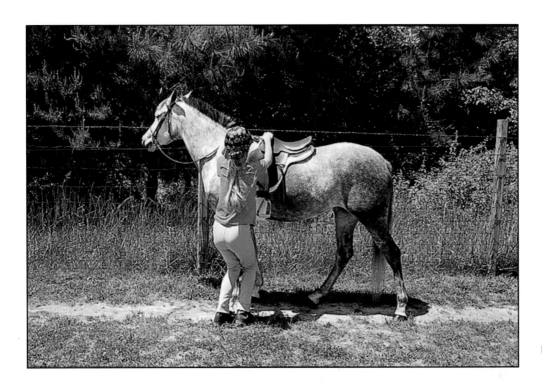

BEND AT THE
KNEES WHEN
YOU LAND!

PERFECT POSITION

Once you have mounted, it's
time to work on your "position"
(the way you sit in the saddle).
Developing a good riding position
is very important. You'll never
improve as a rider if your position
isn't good.

You need to be secure in the
saddle or you could fall off and get
hurt. If you bounce around a lot,
your horse will get grumpy and
misbehave.

A GOOD POSITION.

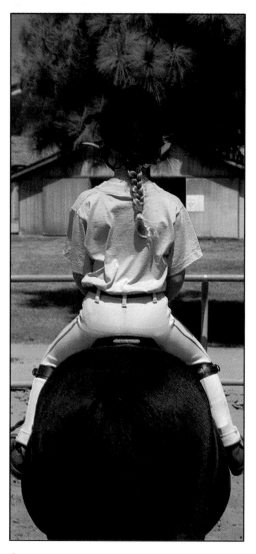

SIT EVENLY ON BOTH SEATBONES.

Head

Hold your head up straight and look forward between your horse's ears. Always look in the direction you are going. If you tip your head down, it affects your balance.

Shoulders

Push your shoulders back and down. Relax. Don't hunch up.

Chest

Keep your upper body straight and upright. Pretend there is a string attached to the top of your head pulling you upward. Stick your chest out a little bit.

Back

Your back should be slightly arched, but don't be stiff. Your back must be flexible and move with the horse.

Take a look at an example of good riding position. Let's start at the top of the body and work our way down.

Seat and Thighs

Sit squarely in the middle of the saddle, which is the lowest part

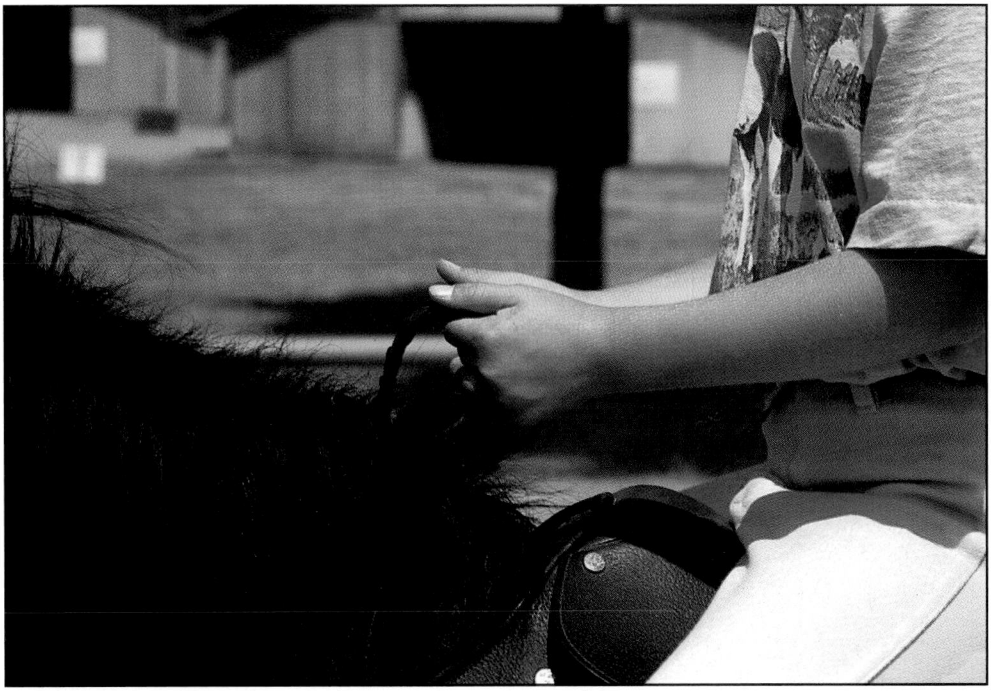

THUMBS UP AT ALL TIMES.

of the seat. Your seat bones (not your whole backside!) must be as close to the saddle as possible, with your body weight evenly distributed.

Hang your legs down naturally and keep your thighs close to the saddle.

Arms

Try to keep your arms glued to your sides. Your elbows should be close to your body. If your arms are in the correct place, you should be able to imagine a straight line all the way from your forearms through the reins to the bit.

Hands

Your hands should be level and your knuckles must face outwards. Your thumbs must be on top of the reins at all times.

NO PUPPY DOG HANDS!

Don't look like a puppy begging for a treat!

Keep your fingers firmly closed around the reins or they could slip out of your hands.

Holding the Reins

When you ride, you use the reins to steer. It's important to hold them correctly or they could slip out of your hands.

The rein should be in the palm of your hand. Close your three middle fingers around the rein and rest your thumb on top of it. Put your pinky finger under the rein. Your palms should face each other and be about an inch or two apart.

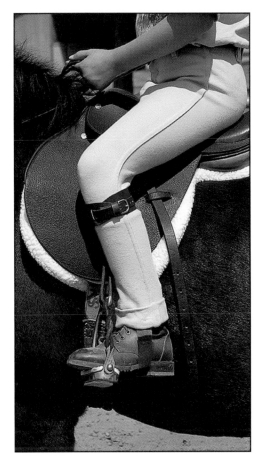

KEEP THOSE HEELS DOWN AND POINT YOUR
TOES FORWARD.

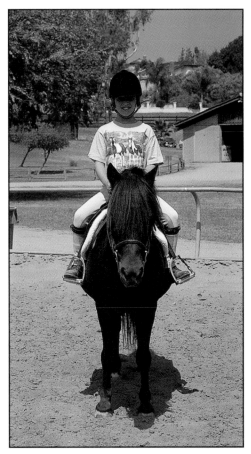

YOUR FEET SHOULD BE EVEN IN THE STIRRUPS.

Legs

Your knees can touch the saddle, but don't grip with them.
Squeezing hard with your knees
throws you forward.

Your lower legs should be
close to your horse's sides, slightly
behind the girth. If you look down,
you should see only the tips of
your toes.

Feet

You've probably heard riding
teachers call out, "Keep those

heels down!" That's because keeping your heels down is essential to a good riding position. Your toes must be higher than your heels. Keep the stirrup under the ball of your foot. Your feet should be even on both sides of the horse.

3 The Walk

When you are learning to ride, you need to start off at the slowest gait: the walk. Once you can control a horse safely at a slow speed, you can move on to more exciting activities.

THE AIDS

First you need to learn about aids. Aids are signals that tell a horse what you want him to do. There are "natural" aids and "artificial" aids.

NATURAL AIDS

Legs: Squeezing your horse's sides with your lower legs can tell him to go forward, sideways, or backwards.

Hands: Your hands hold the reins, which attach to the bit. You use your hands to turn a horse and to slow him down.

Seat: The way you sit affects your horse's movement. When you sit deep in the saddle, he may slow down. Leaning forward tells him to go faster.

Voice: Some horses are trained to obey voice commands. For example, if you say "Whoa," the horse will slow down.

ARTIFICIAL AIDS

Whips: Sometimes you will carry a whip if a horse is lazy. Always hold it in the hand near the inside of the arena. Hold the whip by the handle and let the bottom part rest on your thigh.

Use a whip as little as possible. Only use it when a horse has ignored natural aids, like your legs or voice. Never use a whip on a

horse's head or neck. Give him a tap or two on the area behind the girth. Never lose your temper and beat a horse with a whip!

Spurs: If you are new to riding, you should not wear spurs. Only wear spurs if your instructor tells you to and she teaches you how to

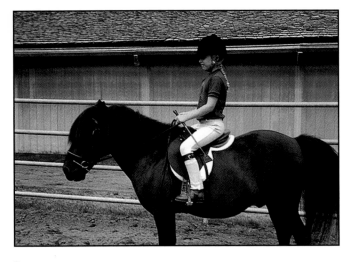

REST A WHIP ON YOUR THIGH.

USE A WHIP BEHIND YOUR LEG.

DON'T USE SPURS UNLESS YOU ARE AN EXPERIENCED RIDER.

use them. If they are not used correctly, they can hurt a horse. Always make sure the spur points downward.

FIRST STEPS!

Before you ask your horse to walk forward, check your position. Is it perfect? Where are your legs? They should be glued to your horse's sides. What about your hands? They should be even with each other and close to the withers. Are you holding the reins correctly? They should be even on both sides. You may have to shorten them by moving your hands further up the reins, closer to your horse's mouth.

When you are ready, look straight ahead and squeeze your horse's sides with your lower legs. Once the horse is walking, keep your legs touching his sides. If he

SQUEEZING WITH YOUR LEGS ASKS YOUR HORSE TO MOVE FORWARD.

slows down, you can squeeze again with your legs to urge him forward. Keep your heels down and toes pointing straight ahead.

As a horse moves, he nods his head. You'll feel this nodding movement with your hands through the reins. Keep your hands flexible and let them follow the horse's movement. Pretend the reins are rubber bands and let your hands give and take with the pressure. This is called having "contact." When an instructor says, "Pick up a contact with the reins," she means shorten your reins and follow the motion of your horse's head. You should have a slight contact at all times.

WRONG!

If the reins are too tight, your horse will think you want him to stop. He will also be uncomfortable with you tugging on the reins

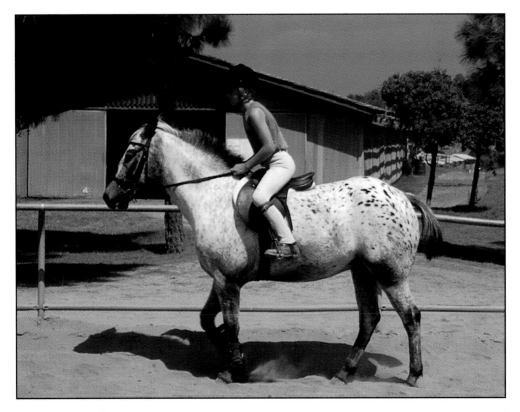

A HORSE DOESN'T LIKE THE REINS TO BE TOO TIGHT.

all the time. If the reins are too loose, however, you have little control over your horse, and it will be difficult to turn or stop him.

KICK! KICK! KICK!

Sometimes it's difficult to get a lazy horse to move. Should you kick him? Some instructors say yes. But too much kicking makes a horse angry and deadens his sides.

If you ride a slow-poke, alternately squeeze with each leg to get him to move (squeeze once with your left leg, then as he steps forward, squeeze him with your right leg). Continue until he moves on. If he *still* ignores you, give him a little kick or two with both feet,

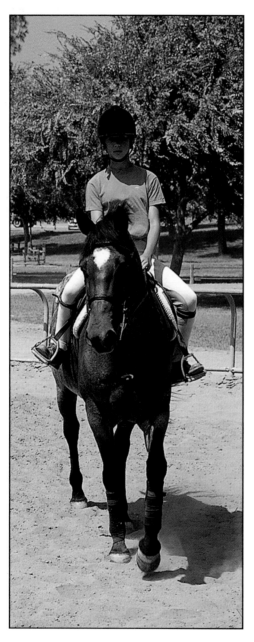

Look where you are going when turning.

or try a flick of the whip behind your leg.

STEERING A HORSE

Once you have your horse walking nicely, it won't be long before you need to turn him. At first, it may seem easy to tug on the rein in the direction you want to go, but this is not correct. You must use both your hands *and* legs to steer a horse.

Before you make your turn, look in the direction you want to go, then ask your horse to turn. If you are turning to the left, use your fingers to squeeze the left rein. You may pull your hand back a tiny bit. Your horse should turn his head slightly to the left. At the same time, keep your left leg next to the girth and move your right leg back a little bit, behind the girth. These aids tell your horse to bend while he is turning.

The horse should bend his body around your left leg. Your right leg, behind the girth, stops him from swinging his hindquarters around and straightening up

YOUR OUTSIDE LEG SHOULD BE BEHIND THE GIRTH.

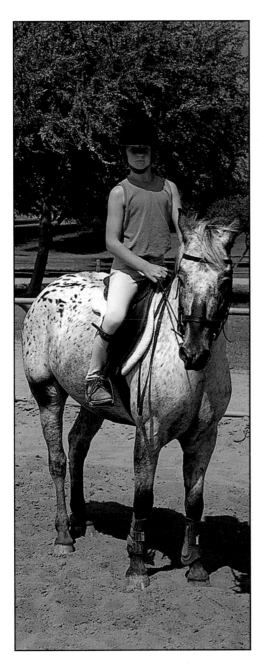

PUT YOUR INSIDE LEG ON THE GIRTH.

again. Once you have turned, stop squeezing on the left rein and move your right leg back to the girth.

If you are turning a horse to the right, squeeze the right rein until he turns his head slightly. Keep your right leg next to the girth and your left leg behind the girth. If you are riding in a circle, think "inside leg next to the girth, outside leg behind the girth" and your horse should bend nicely.

TURNING TIPS

- Always look in the direction you want your horse to go.

DON'T LEAN IN THE DIRECTION YOU WANT TO GO.

When you turn your head, your body weight shifts slightly, giving the horse a signal that you want him to turn.

- Don't lean *too* much. This unbalances your horse and he may turn clumsily.

- Keep your hands close together when turning. Don't lift your turning hand up in the air. If your instructor is watching, she should not be able to tell that you are asking your horse to turn.

WHOA, PLEASE!

Prepare yourself to halt before you give your horse any instructions. Sit deeply on both seat bones in the middle of the saddle's seat. Keep your back straight and look ahead to where you want your horse to halt. Keep your legs touching your horse's sides, but don't squeeze them.

Begin squeezing your fingers around both reins. This puts pressure on the horse's bit and tells him "slow down." Continue

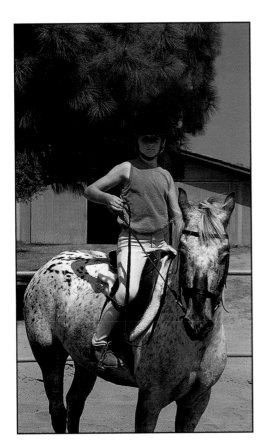

DON'T LIFT YOUR HANDS IN THE AIR WHEN TURNING.

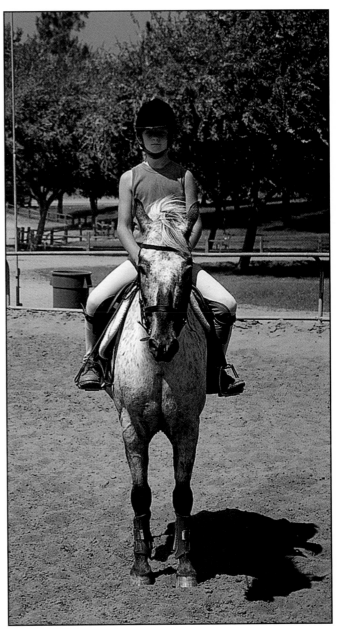

squeezing until he stops. When he halts, relax your hands and stop squeezing immediately.

Pulling steadily on the reins will not stop a horse. In fact, most horses fight against a constant contact and pull against you. Small tugs or squeezes on the reins are more effective than yanking.

WHEN YOUR HORSE HALTS, STOP SQUEEZING THE REINS.

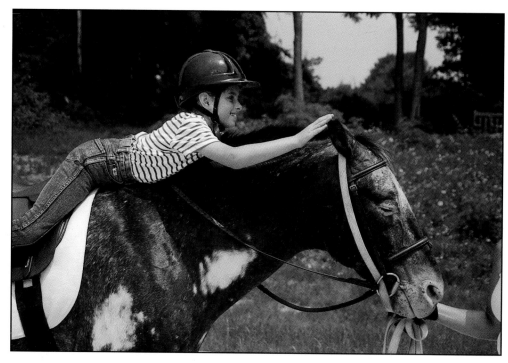

STRETCH FORWARD AND TOUCH YOUR HORSE'S EARS.

EXERCISES

It's a good idea to limber up and get into shape by doing fun exercises in the saddle. They improve your balance and help you relax if you are nervous. Here are some easy exercises you can do to warm up at the beginning of a lesson. Do exercises standing still or at the walk. Tie your reins in a knot so you can steer easily with one hand.

Leaning forward: Hold the reins in one hand and lean forward and touch your horse's ears with the other hand. Keep the lower parts of your legs right by the girth. Don't let them swing backward. Repeat with your other hand.

Arm circles: Hold the reins in one hand and stretch your other hand out horizontally. Make four or five big circles and then do the same with the other hand.

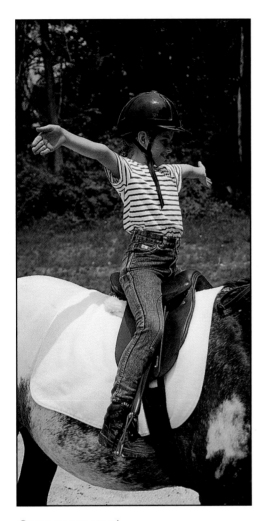

CIRCLE THOSE ARMS!

Toe touches: Hold the reins in your left hand and reach over your horse's neck and touch your left toe with your right hand. Repeat with your other hand and opposite leg.

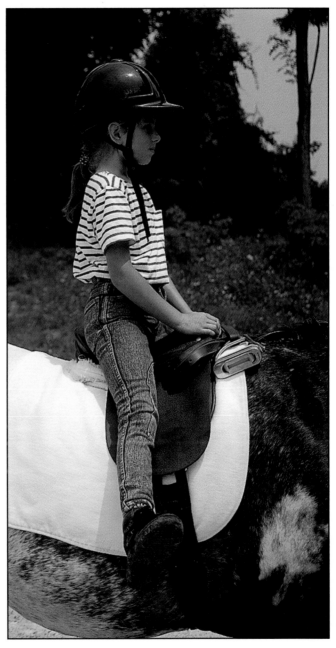

ROTATE THOSE ANKLES!

Ankle twists: Take both feet out of the stirrups and make circles in the air to loosen up your ankle muscles.

Round the world: This exercise is tricky so ask a helper to hold your horse. Take your feet out of the stirrups and drop the reins. Hold the pommel with your right hand and the cantle with your left. Swing your right leg over the horse's withers until you are sitting sidesaddle. Then lift your left leg over the horse's back so you face his tail. Swing your right leg over, too, so you face the other side. Finally, swing your left leg over so you face forward again. Move slowly. You don't want to scare your horse.

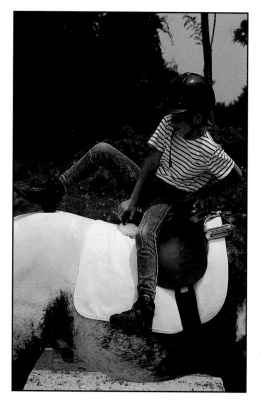

GOING ROUND THE WORLD IS FUN!

4 The Trot

Once you are an expert at walking, turning, and stopping a horse, you are ready for the trot. Trotting is very bumpy! The first time you trot, you may find yourself bouncing around in the saddle and hanging onto the horse's mane so you don't fall off! Don't worry. You'll soon get used to the up-and-down motion of the trot.

Your position at the trot should be just the same as at the walk:

✔ Look in the direction you are going

✔ Elbows close to your body

✔ Hands even and near the withers

✔ Back straight

✔ Sit deep in the saddle with your weight evenly distributed on both seat bones

✔ Lower legs glued to your horse's sides

✔ Heels down and toes pointing forward

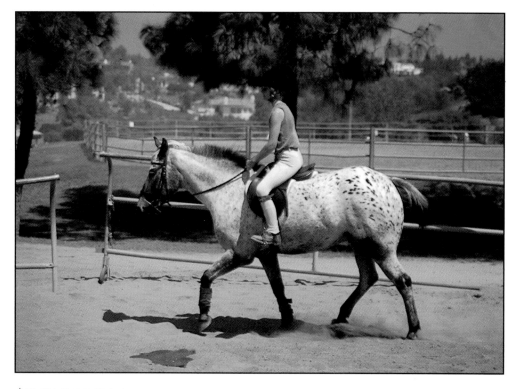

ASK FOR THE TROT FROM AN ENERGETIC WALK.

Before you ask a horse to trot, make sure he is walking along at a nice, steady pace. If he is poking along like a snail with his head on the ground, it is difficult to get him to trot.

TRANSITIONS

During lessons, you may hear your instructor talk about transitions. A transition is simply a change of gait or pace. Going from walk to trot is a transition. So is going from trot to canter.

Your goal as a rider is to make transitions as smooth as possible. When you ask your horse to trot, he should trot right away— it shouldn't take five minutes of kicking. When you are trotting and ask for the walk, you should not have to tug, tug, tug, on the reins to get your horse to slow down.

Prepare for transitions before you ask for them. If you want to slow down, seat yourself deep in the saddle before you squeeze the reins. If you want to speed up, you may need to shorten the reins before you squeeze with your legs.

TROT ON!

When you ask your horse to trot, you may need to shorten your reins slightly. Then squeeze strongly with your legs, and your horse should begin trotting. Once he is trotting, you want him moving forward at a brisk, steady pace. His steps should be regular and even.

POSITION TIPS

• Try to stay relaxed. A relaxed body absorbs the up-and-down motion of the trot. A stiff body bounces around a lot. This can be painful for horse and rider.

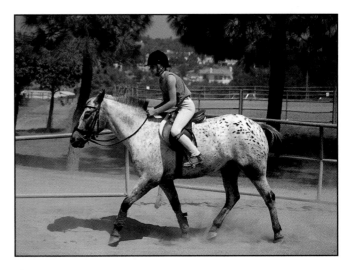

DON'T GRIP WITH YOUR KNEES.

• When you first learn how to trot, it is easy to lean forward and grip with your knees. It feels safer to be out of the bumpy saddle and close to your horse's neck. But this position isn't comfortable for your horse and you'll be unbalanced. If your horse stumbles, you could fall off. Leaning forward also tells your horse to go faster, and you don't want that!

• Don't hang onto the reins with a tight grip. This annoys your horse. Keep your hands still and close to his withers.

If you are bouncing around, hold on to the saddle pommel until you get used to the trot.

POSTING TO THE TROT

Trotting is a lot less bumpy when you learn how to post. Posting means rising up and down in the saddle as a horse trots. It lessens the stress on a horse's back and makes trotting less tiring for you.

When a horse trots, he springs from one diagonal pair of legs to the other. For example, his front right leg and his back left leg move forward together. Then the front left leg and back right leg move together. There is a moment of suspension between each step and this is why the trot is so bouncy.

When you post, you rise out of the saddle when one diagonal pair of legs springs off the ground, and

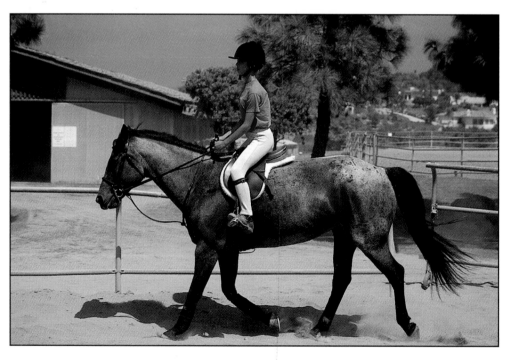

SIT IN THE SADDLE WHEN THE HORSE'S OUTSIDE FRONT LEG IS UNDERNEATH HIM.

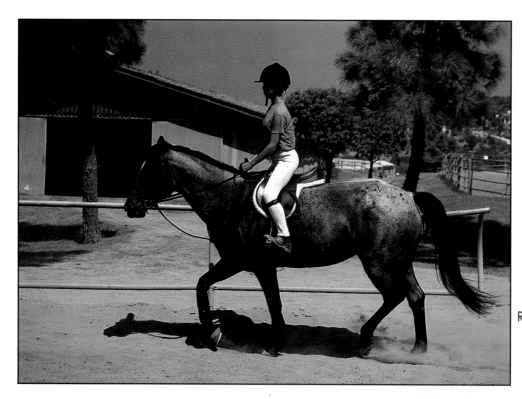

RISE OUT OF THE SADDLE WHEN THE OUTSIDE FRONT LEG IS FORWARD.

sit down as the same pair returns to the ground. The movement of the horse actually bounces you forward and slightly out of the saddle, making posting easier. But stay close to the saddle. Don't bounce two feet in the air!

Sometimes posting is easier if you count one-two, one-two, as your horse trots. Do this until you can feel a rhythm. Rise and sit down in time with the horse's trot. Rise on "one" and sit on "two." It

AND BACK DOWN AGAIN.

41

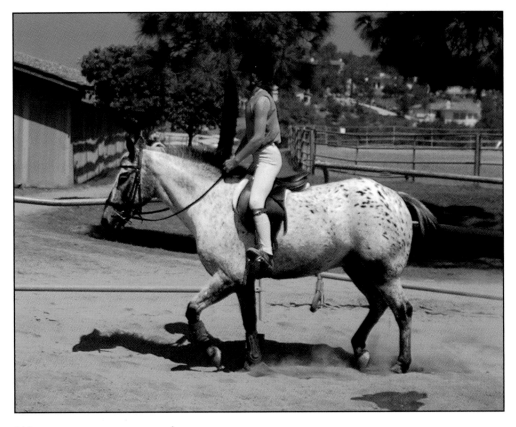

WHOOPS—WRONG DIAGONAL!

will take a little practice, but you'll get it!

PRACTICE MAKES PERFECT

You can practice posting while your horse is standing still or walking. As you rise, push down on the stirrups with your heels. Then slowly sink back into the saddle. Be careful not to bang down on your horse's back.

DIAGONALS

Once you can post at the trot, you need to learn about "diagonals." When an instructor says, "Check your diagonal," it means that she wants you to check that you are rising and sitting as you should be. If you are on the correct diagonal, it is easier for your horse to stay balanced as he trots around the ring.

If you are riding around the ring on the right rein (your right hand is on the inside), you should be rising and sitting in time with your horse's left foreleg, the one on the outside of the arena. If you are riding on the left rein, you should be rising and sitting in time with your horse's right foreleg.

Check Your Diagonal

There is an easy way to tell if you are on the correct diagonal. Lower your eyes (not your whole head, because this affects your balance) and look at your horse's outside foreleg. When it is forward, you should be up in the air. When it is back under your horse, you should be sitting.

When you change direction, you must change your diagonal, too. This is also easy. When you are trotting in the other direction, simply sit in the saddle for

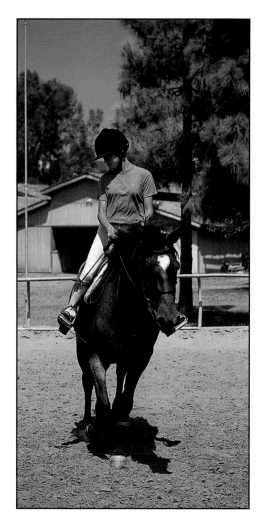

DON'T TILT YOUR WHOLE HEAD TO CHECK THE DIAGONAL. JUST LOWER YOUR EYES.

two beats (say to yourself: up-down, up-**down, down**-up), then rise again. You should be on the correct diagonal. If you aren't, sit down another two beats, then rise.

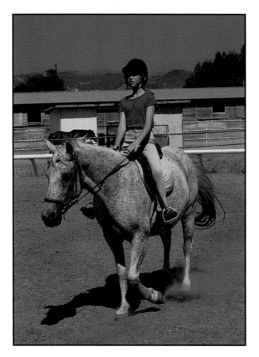

TRY TO RELAX DURING THE SITTING TROT.

Diagonal Tips

If you are on a trail ride and there is no inside or outside rein, you should still change your diagonal once in a while. This will keep your horse flexible, and he won't get too used to one diagonal. Some horses are more comfortable to ride on one diagonal than the other, but you must still change diagonals regularly.

THE SITTING TROT

When you ride a sitting trot, you don't rise. Your instructor will make you do the sitting trot because it's a good way of learning how to balance on a horse. It also strengthens the muscles you need for riding. The sitting trot is tiring for you and your horse, so only do it for a few minutes.

It's important to relax during the sitting trot and let your whole body absorb the bumpy movement. Sit deep in the saddle and keep your back straight. Stretch your legs down and keep them close to your horse's sides. Hold onto the pommel if you think you might fall off.

5 The Canter and Gallop

If you feel secure in the saddle at the trot, it's time to try the canter. The canter is smoother than the trot and the feeling is very pleasant. When your horse canters, his hind legs push off the ground together and he rocks backward and forward in a rhythm (and so do you).

PREPARING TO CANTER

The canter is faster than the trot, so you must be in control of your horse before you ask him to move up a gear. It is best to learn how to canter in a ring, not out on a trail.

Ask your horse to trot and make sure that he is moving forward briskly. If he's poking along slowly, it will be hard to get him to canter. It is easiest to ask for canter when you are doing a sitting trot. Sit deep in the saddle and take a firm contact on the reins. Keep your back straight and look ahead.

LEADS

Ask for the canter when your horse is trotting in a circle or around a bend in the arena. Why? Because it is more likely side foreleg. The inside foreleg is sometimes called the "leading leg." He will be more balanced if he is on the correct lead.

TAKEOFF

When you reach the bend in the arena, give the aids for canter:

✔ Sit deep in the saddle

✔ Heels down, toes pointing forward

✔ Keep your inside leg next to the girth

✔ Press your outside leg on your horse's side, behind the girth

✔ Squeeze his side with your outside leg. If he ignores you, give him a nudge or small kick with your outside leg

When your horse takes off, it feels as if he is leaping into the

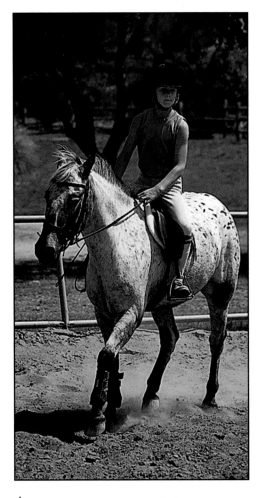

ASK FOR THE CANTER ON A BEND.

that he will pick up the correct "lead" when he is on a curve. What is a "lead"? When your horse canters, his inside foreleg should reach further forward than his out-

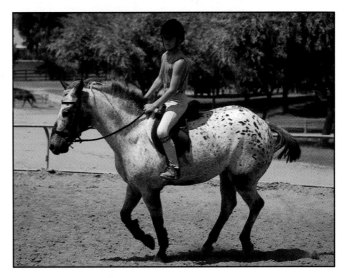

THE HORSE'S INSIDE LEG SHOULD LEAD.

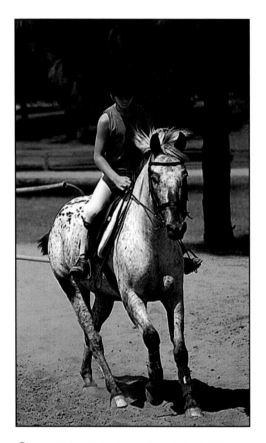

GLANCE DOWN TO SEE IF YOU ARE ON THE CORRECT LEAD.

the motion of your horse's head and neck.

Check that your horse is on the correct lead. Lower your eyes to look at his inside foreleg. It should reach out further than the outside leg. Do not tip your whole head, though, because this can unbalance your horse.

When you are more experienced, you will be able to "feel" when your horse is on the wrong lead, because the canter will seem clumsy or stiff. If he takes off on the wrong lead, ask him to trot again. Sit back in the saddle, move both of your legs back to the girth, and stop squeezing. Then squeeze the reins until he slows down. When you get back to trot, give the aids for canter again.

POSITION TIPS

- Don't lean to the inside when asking your horse to canter. This can unbalance him and make it hard for him to pick up the correct lead.

- Don't let your hands be stiff. If you are constantly tugging on

air. Keeping your legs firmly in place on his sides will help you keep your balance. Press your seat bones into the saddle and follow the horse's rocking movement with your body. Relax. Cantering is fun!

Just as you do at the walk, let your hands and the reins follow

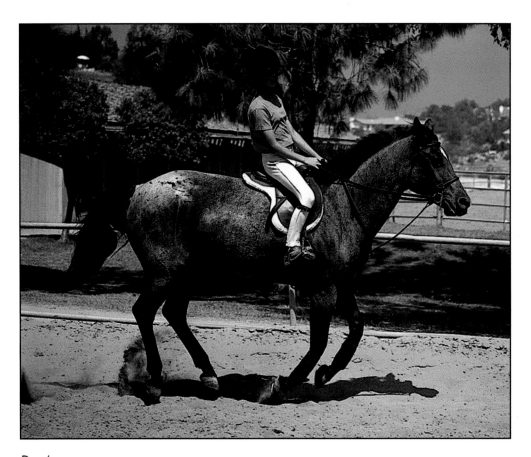

DON'T GET LEFT BEHIND AT THE CANTER.

the reins, your horse may think you want him to slow down.

- Try not to get left behind your horse's rocking motion when you are cantering. Sitting too far back in the saddle makes your legs fly forward; you won't be secure, and this also hurts your horse's back.

THE GALLOP

The gallop is the horse's fastest speed, and for a new rider it is very exciting. The gallop is faster than the canter because the horse takes bigger strides. While he races along, he stretches out his head, neck, and body as far as he can.

49

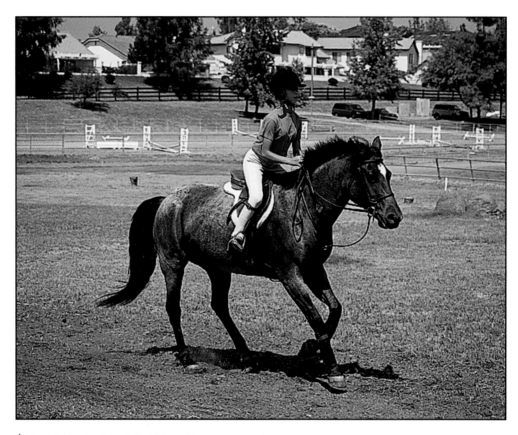

LEAN FORWARD AND OUT OF THE SADDLE AT THE GALLOP.

Galloping is fun, but it can be dangerous if you aren't very experienced. You must be able to control your horse at a canter before you gallop. Some horses take advantage of you at the gallop and tear off at top speed wherever they want! Practice galloping in an enclosed ring before you try it out on a trail or in a big field.

Preparing to Gallop

Once your horse is cantering, shorten your reins and squeeze with your legs until he picks up speed. Push your heels down and get up in "galloping position." Keep the lower part of your legs next to your horse's sides and lift your seat slightly out of the saddle. Tilt your upper body slightly forward and closer to your horse's neck. Lifting your weight off your horse's back lets him go faster.

Move your hands a little higher up his neck and let them follow the movement of his head as it stretches forward with each stride.

When you want to slow down, sit back in the saddle, keep your legs on your horse's sides, and squeeze on both reins. When he slows down, give him a big pat or two to let him know you are pleased with him.

POSITION TIPS

- Don't let your arms and legs flap around when galloping. It is fun zooming along, but don't forget your position. Keep your elbows next to your body and glue those legs to your horse's sides.

- Try not to grip the saddle with your knees. If you do, your lower legs will automatically shoot back and you will not be secure in the saddle. If your horse stumbles, you'll take a dive!

IMPROVE YOUR POSITION

Before you can think about jumping, your position must be perfect. Riding without stirrups and riding bareback will improve your position.

Riding without stirrups can be hard work, but it is a super way to

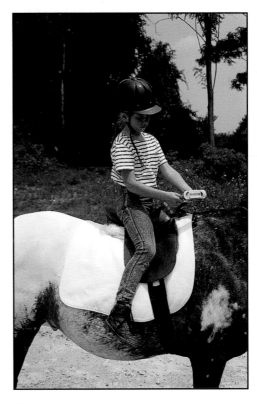

CROSS YOUR STIRRUPS IN FRONT OF THE SADDLE.

51

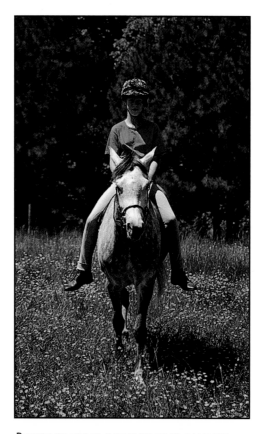

BAREBACK RIDING IMPROVES YOUR BALANCE.

strengthen your legs and make you more secure in the saddle. Try to ride without stirrups for a short while every day.

Cross your stirrups over the saddle so they don't bang your horse's sides. Try to relax and sit as quietly as you can in the saddle. Begin with the walk. When you feel confident, you can try the trot and canter. Try posting without stirrups. It may tire you out, but you can do it!

Riding bareback is lots of fun. Stay in an enclosed space (a ring) in case you slide off and your horse keeps going. Riding bareback helps you to improve your balance. When you ride bareback, always wear a helmet and always use a bridle on your horse.

6 Jumping

It takes lots of practice in the saddle at the walk, trot, and canter before you can jump. Why? Because you need to be perfectly balanced and safe on your horse's back before you begin popping over fences. When a horse jumps he leaps up into the air, and if you are not 100 percent secure in the saddle, you could fall off.

SHORTEN YOUR STIRRUPS

The first thing you must do before jumping is shorten your stirrups about two holes. This allows you to bring your body weight forward so that you can stay over your horse's center of balance throughout the jump.

JUMPING POSITION

Before you jump over your first fence, you must get into jumping position (sometimes called "forward position"). When you are in jumping position, you lean forward over your horse's

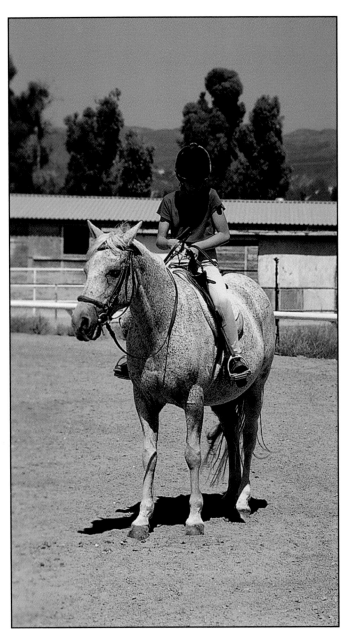

SHORTEN YOUR STIRRUPS FOR JUMPING.

neck. Sitting like this helps you stay balanced, and lets you move with your horse as he clears a fence. Jumping position makes it easier for your horse to jump because you don't bounce around on his back.

Let's take a look at the correct jumping position.

Head

Hold your head up high and look straight ahead. Looking down affects your balance.

Shoulders

Keep your shoulders back and down. Don't slouch!

Chest and Back

Your upper body and chest should bend forward over your horse's neck. Stick your chest out a little bit. Your back should be flat and straight, not rounded.

Arms

Push your arms forward so that your elbows are in front of your body instead of glued to your

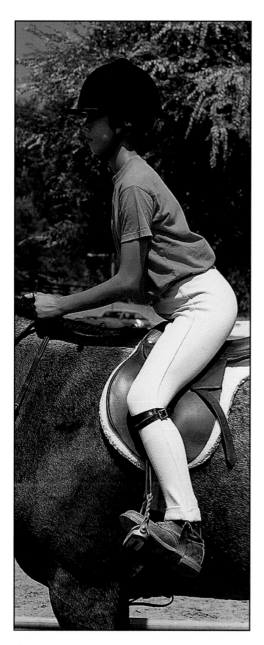

A GOOD JUMPING POSITION.

sides. Bend your arms at the elbows, and imagine a straight line running all the way from your elbow down the rein to your horse's mouth.

Hands

Make sure your hands are level and as close together as possible. Keep your thumbs facing upward.

Maintain a firm grip on the reins by keeping your fingers closed. Your reins need to be shortened for jumping, but your hands should still follow the motion of your horse's neck and head.

When you are learning to jump, it's a good idea to push your hands forward when going over a fence. Rest your hands on your horse's neck, about 8 to 10 inches in front of the saddle. If you do this, the reins become looser and you won't jab your horse in the mouth if you get left behind the motion. Pushing your hands forward is sometimes called a "quick release."

Hips and Seat

Bend your upper body forward from your hips, not your waist. Push your bottom back a bit. Raise it slightly out of the saddle, but keep it close enough so that you can sit back down quickly and get into your regular riding position.

Thighs

Keep your thighs close to the saddle. Bend at your knees and let them touch the saddle flap.

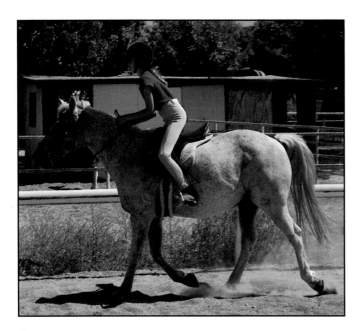

PRACTICE THE JUMPING POSITION.

Lower Legs

Your lower legs must be underneath you, close to the girth. Keep a strong contact with your horse's sides so that you can ask him to move forward. Your legs must stay in this position, even when you are flying over a fence.

Keep your ankles flexible. They are shock absorbers for the rest of your body.

Feet

Place the ball of your foot (the widest part) on the stirrup pad and push your heels down lower than your toes.

PRACTICE!

Practice the jumping position at the walk, trot, and canter. Stay in the position for a few minutes and then sit down and rest. The jumping position is tiring because you are really working your leg muscles hard.

TROTTING POLES

You might want to jump over a big fence right away, but starting small will make you a better rider. Start out by riding over trotting poles. They will help you practice your jumping position and improve your balance.

Use at least four or five trotting poles and place them parallel to each other, across your path.

Pony poles: If you are riding a pony, place the poles about three

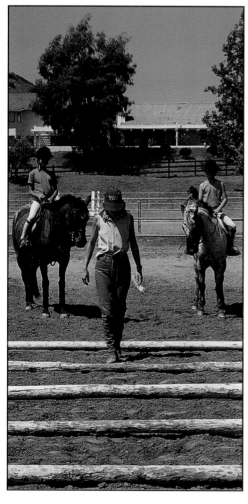

MAKE SURE TROTTING POLES ARE CORRECTLY SPACED FOR YOUR HORSE OR PONY.

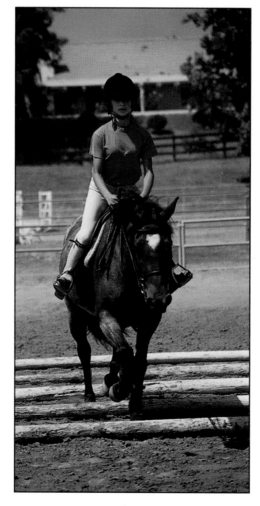

STAY IN THE JUMPING POSITION OVER THE POLES.

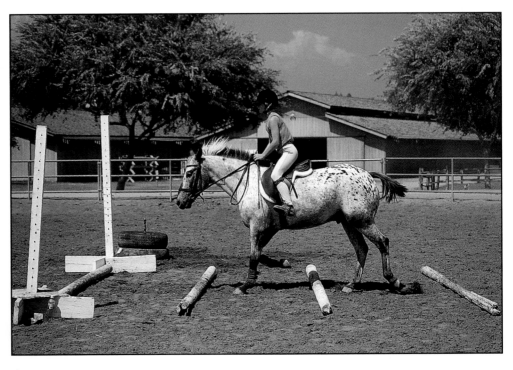

ALWAYS LOOK STRAIGHT AHEAD.

and a half to four feet (1.2m) apart. If they are farther apart, the pony may trip.

Horse poles: If you are riding a horse, place the poles about four and a half to five feet apart (1.5m).

Once the poles are set, ask your horse to trot forward at a steady, active pace. He should not be moving slowly. When he is trotting nicely, you can get into jumping position. Give yourself plenty of room to approach the poles.

Don't yank your horse into them at the last second.

Here are some things to think about when going over poles.

✔ Make your horse trot over all the poles. Keep your legs on his sides, squeezing to keep him moving forward. If he slows down, he could trip.

✔ Put your hands slightly up on the horse's neck in a quick release.

✔ Maintain a firm grip on the reins. Squeeze them if your horse speeds up too much. He should not canter over trotting poles!

✔ Aim for the center of the poles.

✔ Look straight ahead.

✔ Try to relax and absorb the bumpy motion with your knees and ankles.

✔ When you finish jumping the poles, keep trotting forward. Don't stop right away.

✔ Trot over the poles in both directions so that your horse doesn't get bored.

HANG ON!

Use a neck strap if it is hard to stay balanced when jumping. Fasten a stirrup leather around your horse's neck like a collar (but not too tight!), and hang on to it to stop yourself from bouncing around. If you don't have a neck strap, grab a handful of mane. It is better to hold onto a neck strap or mane than to grab the reins and yank on your horse's mouth if you lose your balance.

YOUR FIRST JUMP

If you are new to riding, the best way to jump your first fence is to place a small cross-rail about three yards after a line of trotting poles. The cross-rail fence should not be too big—only about a foot and a half above the ground.

Popping over this first fence will be easy because you are

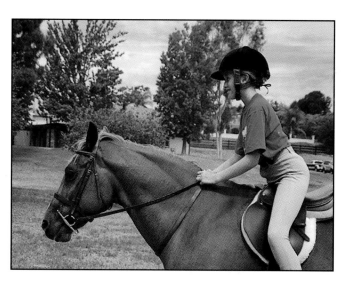

GRAB HOLD OF A NECK STRAP WHEN LEARNING HOW TO JUMP.

already in jumping position after the trotting poles. Also, your horse should still be moving forward in a nice, active rhythm, so it will be simple for him to jump the fence.

Ask your horse to trot at a brisk pace, then head for the trotting poles. Remember to:

✔ Get into jumping position.

✔ Push your hands forward in a quick release. Grab some mane.

✔ Keep your heels down and your legs glued to your horse's sides.

✔ Aim for the middle of the poles.

✔ Look straight ahead at the cross-rail fence and trot on over the poles.

When you are finished with the trotting poles, stay in jumping position and steer your horse to the middle of the cross-rails. Use your legs to keep him moving forward. He should jump the X part where the poles cross.

When you are safely on the other side of the fence, sit back in the saddle and take up your normal riding position. Well done! Be sure to give your horse a big pat.

A SINGLE FENCE

Once you have mastered trotting poles and a small cross-pole jump, ask your instructor to watch you try a single fence called a "simple vertical." Place one pole about two feet off the ground, with a second pole on the ground slightly in front of it. The ground pole helps a horse know where he should take off.

It may be difficult to keep your horse going forward at a nice pace without the trotting poles, so be sure to get him moving with your legs **before** you head toward the jump.

Circle once or twice before approaching the fence to make sure your horse is trotting actively, then aim toward the center. Get into jumping position a few yards in front of the fence and grab some mane. Push your heels down

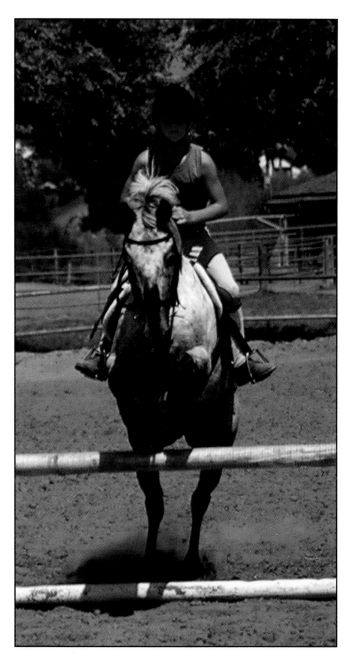

AIM FOR THE MIDDLE OF THE X.

ASK YOUR HORSE TO MOVE BRISKLY TOWARD A VERTICAL FENCE.

A GOOD JUMPING POSITION.

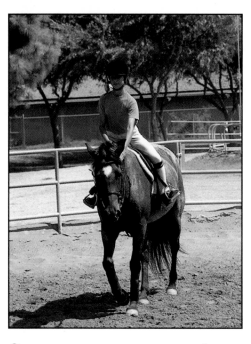

GIVE YOUR HORSE A PAT IF HE IS GOOD!

and squeeze with your lower legs until your horse clears the fence.

When he lands, keep your legs on his sides and sit back down in the saddle. Again, pat your horse so that he knows he's done a great job.

JUMPING PROBLEMS

Several things can go wrong when you jump. Let's look at some typical situations.

Refusals

A refusal means that a horse doesn't want to jump a fence, and

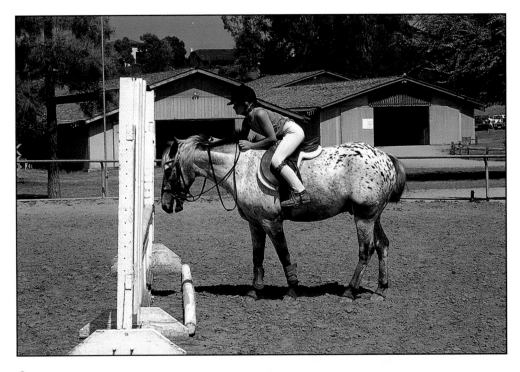

STOPPING IN FRONT OF A FENCE IS CALLED A REFUSAL.

stops in front of it. There are several reasons why a horse may refuse.

- **He may not have jumped very much and is confused or scared:** If a horse does not know how to jump, you must work with trotting poles and low fences until he gains confidence.

- **He is being naughty and stubborn:** If your instructor thinks your horse is misbehaving, you may need to carry a whip and give him a sharp tap behind your leg if he stops in front of a fence.

- **You are not secure in the saddle:** Most refusals are caused by riders flopping around on a horse's back, unbalancing him.

- **You feel nervous:** A horse can tell if you are scared. If he thinks you don't want to jump a fence, he won't want to jump either! Be brave when jumping.

Use lots of leg on a horse that refuses. Sit deeply in the saddle and make him move toward the fence. Get into jumping position right in front of the fence, and squeeze with your legs to tell your horse to take off. You can't be a wishy-washy rider on a refuser!

Runouts

Sometimes a horse runs out to one side of the fence so he doesn't have to jump. If your horse does this, take a strong contact on the reins when approaching a fence. Always steer him to the middle of the fence and squeeze strongly with your legs.

If your horse likes to dart out to the right, use a strong left rein and squeeze with your right

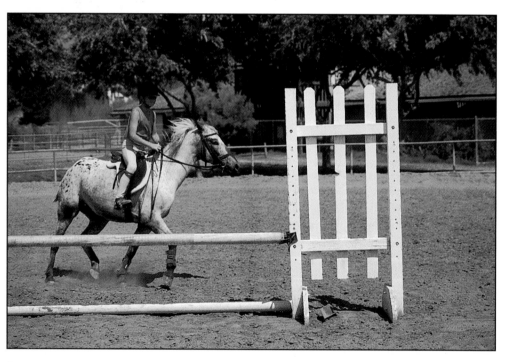

RUNNING OUT HAPPENS WHEN YOU AREN'T STEERING!

leg. If he nips out to the left, tug on the right rein several times and squeeze him with your left leg.

Looking Down

Don't look down at your horse's neck when jumping. Looking down causes problems when you land, because you aren't paying attention to where you are going. It also makes you hunch your back and ruins your position. Look straight ahead, between your horse's ears.

Getting Left Behind

If you don't stay with your horse's motion as he jumps, and end up with plenty of air between you and the saddle, it's called getting left behind. This isn't nice for you or your horse because you land back in the saddle with a BIG BUMP!

You may get left behind if you are not in a secure jumping position when your horse takes off, or if he jumps extra high over a small fence. You shouldn't

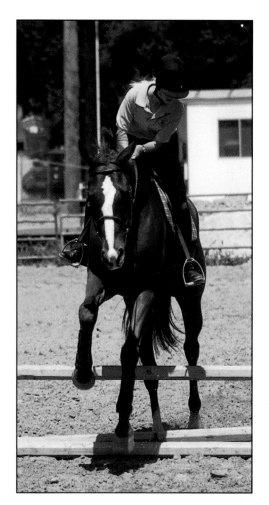

DUCKING UNBALANCES YOUR HORSE.

get left behind if you hold onto a neck strap or some of his mane.

Ducking

Ducking is when a rider leans to one side when jumping a fence. It

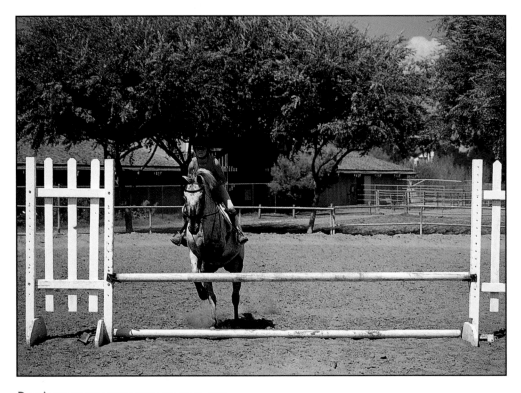

DON'T LET YOUR HORSE VEER TO ONE SIDE.

is a bad habit and can unbalance your horse and make him jump badly. If your instructor says you are ducking, you must concentrate harder on keeping your upper body close to your horse's neck when he jumps.

Jumping to One Side

Always steer your horse to the center of the fence every time you jump. Don't let your horse swerve to one side, because it will be easier for him to run out.

Leaning Too Far Forward

Just because you love jumping doesn't mean you should leap over the fence before your horse! Leaning too far forward makes it hard for him to jump. When you do this, your lower legs go back and your heels come up. If you are in this position when your horse refuses, you will fly over his head!

To avoid this problem, push your heels down, set your legs next to the girth, and keep your bottom close to the saddle. Let the fence come to you instead of trying to anticipate your horse's takeoff.

7 Horse and Pony Problems

Very few horses and ponies are 100 percent perfect. Like people, they often have a bad habit or two. Some horse habits, like sneaking mouthfuls of grass, are not too serious. But others, like bucking or rearing, are dangerous and could hurt you.

If your horse is normally well behaved but suddenly develops a bad habit, don't panic. You may be able to solve the problem yourself. Here are some reasons why a horse is naughty:

- **His tack does not fit properly.** If the saddle is pinching his withers, your horse will be unhappy and may buck or rear. If his bit is too low, it may bang against his teeth and upset him. Check your tack to make sure it fits.

- **He's not feeling well.** A sick horse may be unwilling to work. Ask a vet to look at your horse to see if she can find something wrong with him. A sore leg or tooth can make a horse grumpy.

IS THE SADDLE HURTING YOUR HORSE?

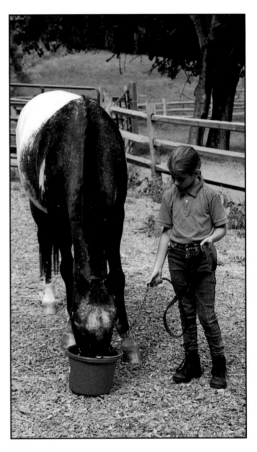

ARE YOU FEEDING YOUR HORSE TOO MUCH HIGH-ENERGY FOOD?

- **Too much feed and too little work.** A horse that is given too much high-energy food and doesn't do enough work will be frisky. If your horse is rambunctious, give him a low-energy feed (one without oats). Let him spend lots of time out in the field so he can get rid of excess energy by running around.

- **Rider problems.** Often a horse misbehaves because of bad riding. Bouncing around on his back makes him sore, and so he may buck. Yanking on his mouth could make him rear.

If you are having problems with your horse, regular lessons are a must.

FALLING OFF

Even top show jumpers fall off occasionally. If you find yourself flying through the air, here

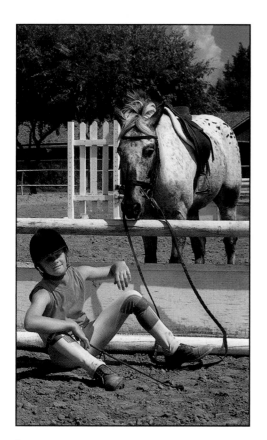

LET GO OF THE REINS IF YOU FALL OFF.

are two things you should try to remember:

1. Let go of the reins! If you hang on to them, you could get dragged along by the horse and he may step on you. Your horse probably won't go too far without you, so let go. It is better to have broken reins than a broken arm.

2. Try to curl up into a tight ball as you fall. Don't hold your arms out to break your fall. The only thing you will break is an arm! Keep both arms close to your sides and roll when you hit the ground.

BUCKING

When a horse bucks he puts his head down, arches his back, and kicks his hind legs in the air. A horse may buck if his saddle is pinching him or if he has excess energy.

If your horse puts his head down and you think he's going to buck, the best thing to do is tug on the reins to get his head up and kick him to get him moving forward. It is hard for a horse to buck if he is moving.

Sit deeply in the saddle. If you lean forward, you will end up on the ground. Don't whack your horse with a whip if he bucks. Ignore bucking and keep him working.

BOLTING

When a horse gallops off at top speed, it is called bolting. A horse may bolt because he is scared or overly excited. Bolting is scary, but you must keep calm so that you can stop him as soon as possible.

Use a "pulley rein" to get your horse to stop.

1. Sit deeply in the saddle.

2. Shorten your reins.

3. Put one hand on the horse's withers and pull back with the other hand. Give the rein a good tug. Continue pulling on one rein until he turns his head

PULL ON ONE REIN AND THEN THE OTHER TO STOP A BOLTER.

toward you. If he won't turn, try the other rein.

4. Then circle, circle, circle! It's hard for a horse to gallop when he is going in a circle. Make the circles smaller and smaller until he slows down.

REARING

Rearing is when a horse stands up on his hind legs. It is very dangerous. If your horse rears a lot, you should sell him—he is not a suitable horse for a young person.

A horse may rear because he doesn't want to move forward. Unfortunately, once a horse learns that rearing is a good way to get out of work it is almost impossible to get him to stop.

Never pull back on the reins if your horse rears. You'll unbalance him and he could fall backwards on top of you.

You should loosen the reins, lean forward, and wrap your arms around his neck. When he lands, kick him so that he moves forward. He can't rear if he is moving.

GRABBING GRASS

It is annoying when you are riding and your horse puts his head down to munch on grass. Use grass reins on a "grass grabber."

It is easy to make grass reins. Tie a long piece of twine to each bit ring. Then run the twine up alongside the cheekpiece and through the browband loop.

Finally, tie the twine to the metal D-rings on each side of the

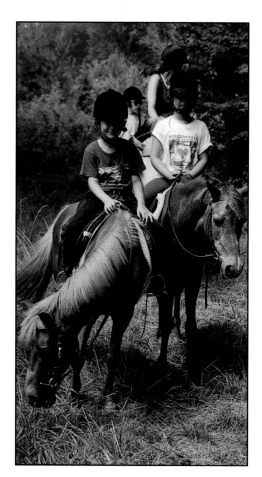

DON'T LET YOUR HORSE EAT WHILE YOU ARE RIDING.

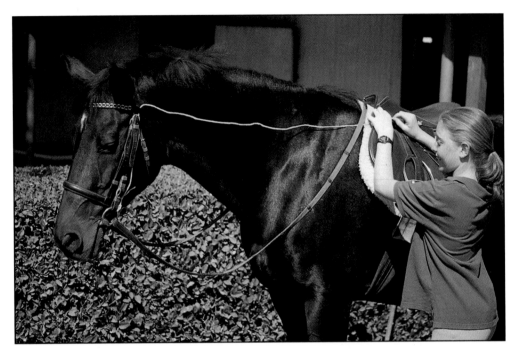

GRASS REINS WILL KEEP A HORSE FROM GRAZING.

saddle. The twine should be short enough to keep your horse from putting his head down to graze, but long enough so that he can bob his head freely as he moves.

KICKING

Be especially careful around a horse that kicks. That means stay away from his hindquarters!

If you have a horse that kicks other horses, you must let everyone who is riding near you

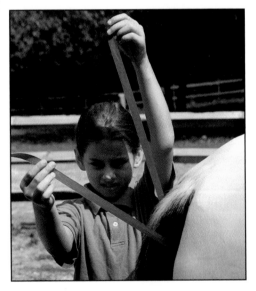

TIE A RED RIBBON ON A KICKER'S TAIL.

74

know about his problem so they can give him plenty of room. If your horse is aggressive to another horse, give him a hard tap behind your leg and ask him to move forward. If he is working, he won't have time to think about kicking.

If you are going to a show or are out on a trail, tie a red ribbon on your horse's tail. This warns other riders that your horse kicks.

8 Fun Activities

Once you feel 100 percent secure in the saddle, you'll discover that there are lots of fun things that you and your horse can do together. There is more to riding than trotting around a ring! Let's look at some activities that will keep you and your horse busy.

TRAIL RIDING

There is nothing like riding out in the open with your horse! Riding on trails in the woods or across fields is lots of fun. It is good exercise for your horse and gives him a break from schooling. Try to get out of the ring as much as you can.

But before you head out, make sure that you are in control of your horse. Even the quietest horse can get excited when he is out in the open, and some horses may buck or bolt.

Part of the fun of trail riding is admiring the scenery, but you must pay attention to what your horse is doing and what's going on around you. Your horse could trip and you could take a tumble. Watch out for trash that might spook your horse.

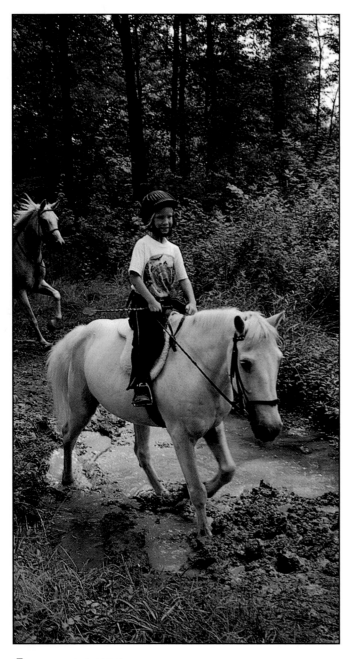

TRAIL RIDING IS GREAT FUN.

If there is a strange-looking object in your path, keep a contact on the reins, squeeze your horse's sides with your legs and tell him to walk forward. Be firm and make him pass the "scary monster"!

Here are some tips to remember when trail riding:

- Always trail ride with a friend. If you are alone and fall off, you could be in big trouble.

- Tell an adult where you are going.

- Carry some change with you so that you can make a phone call if you get in a jam.

- Carry a hoofpick. Rocks or mud in your horse's hooves could make him lame.

- Don't ride along with loose reins. Your position should never be sloppy, but exactly the same as it is in the ring.

- If you ride on other people's land, stick to the trail. Don't ride over crops or get near cattle or other livestock.

- Cantering in a group can excite your horse and he may get out of control. Only canter or gallop if you can stop your horse quickly.

- If you are going to jump over an obstacle, look on the other side before you leap. There may be a hole or something that could trip your horse.

- Always walk back to the barn after a ride. If you always return at top speed, your horse will jog when you try to make him walk slowly.

PONY CLUB

If you are a horse owner, it is a good idea to join the local branch of the Pony Club. There are over 500 Pony Clubs in the United States. Write or call the national office (see page 86) to find out if there is a club in your area. If you live in Canada, see page 86 for the address and phone number of the Canadian Pony Club. Pony Club is for those who are serious about riding and learning about horses.

LOOK BEFORE YOU LEAP.

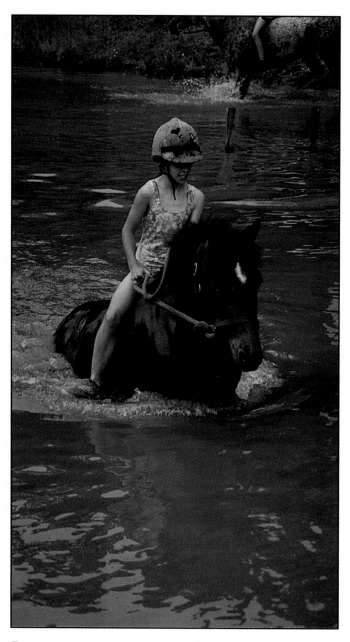

TRY NEW THINGS LIKE SWIMMING AT PONY CLUB CAMP.

You have to be under twenty-one to join, and your parents must be willing to help out.

Your horse doesn't have to be the fanciest in the barn. Horses and ponies of many different shapes, sizes, and breeds are welcome in Pony Club.

Once you are a member, you go to meetings and learn about feeding, shoeing, veterinary care, and other horse-care topics. Pony Club instructors give you lessons and help you train your horse. Pony Club has regular "rallies" to test you on what you learn. If you are a member, you'll have the chance to try different sports, like polo and vaulting.

Each summer, most clubs have a week-long camp where kids do exciting things like taking their horses swimming. It's wonderful to be with lots of other horsey kids!

4-H

There are 4-H clubs in most counties throughout the United States. The 4-H is run by your local agricultural extension office. Check

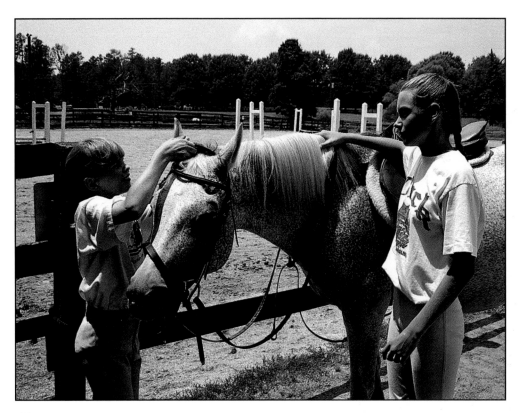

4-H TEACHES YOU ABOUT HORSE CARE.

the telephone book for their number. 4-H members don't always have their own horses. However, many members ride at riding schools and have access to horses. The clubs usually include both English and western riders.

Like Pony Club, 4-H holds training sessions to teach youngsters about riding and horse care. 4-H clubs often have a big, statewide show so that kids from different areas can get together and show off their horses and knowledge.

SHOWING

Taking your horse to a show is a great way to let everyone see how well you have trained him. You might even come home with a

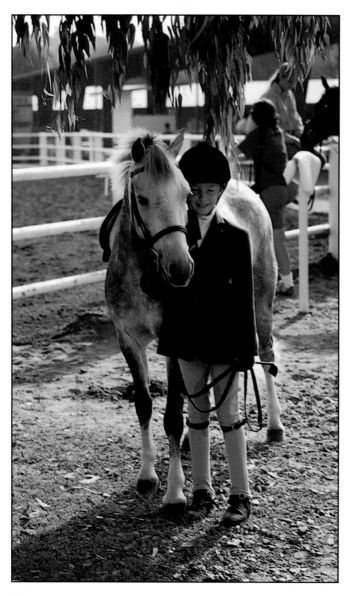

YOU MAY HAVE TO WEAR FORMAL RIDING CLOTHES TO A SHOW.

ribbon or two! Horse shows take place all year round.

To find out about shows in your area, ask your instructor or look on the bulletin board in a local tack shop. Some of the classes offered may suit your horse. You can enter flat classes or jumping classes. There are breed classes, too.

Usually you are required to wear more formal riding clothes when you go to a show than when you are schooling. You may have to wear a dark riding jacket with long sleeves. Your horse must be groomed until he shines, and your tack must be in perfect order, too.

It is very important that your horse is well mannered at home before you take him to a show. If your horse misbehaves in the ring, the judge won't like it and you will feel embarrassed.

If you like showing, you may want to join the American Horse Shows Association (AHSA). See page 85 for their address and telephone number.

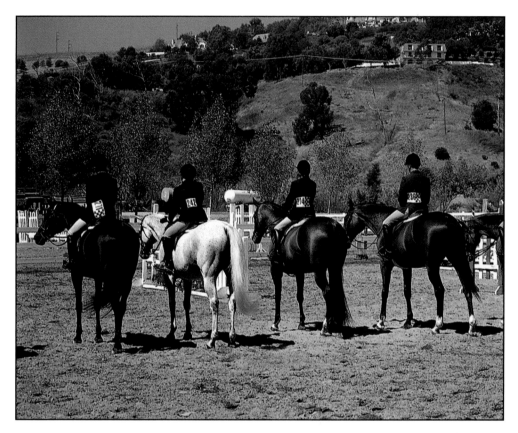

YOUR HORSE MUST BE WELL BEHAVED BEFORE GOING TO A SHOW.

American Camping
Association
800-777-CAMP

American Connemara
Pony Society
2630 Hunting Ridge Road
Winchester, VA 22603
540-662-5953

American Horse Council
1700 K Street NW
Suite 300
Washington, DC 20006-3805
202-296-4031

American Horse Shows
Association
220 East 42nd Street
Suite 409
New York, NY 10017
212-972-2472

American Morgan Horse
Association
P.O. Box 960
Shelburne, VT 05482-0960
802-985-4944

American Quarter Horse
Association
P.O. Box 200
Amarillo, TX 79168
806-376-4811

American Riding Instructors
Association
P.O. Box 282
Alton Bay, NH 03810-0282
603-875-4000

American Quarter Horse
Association
P.O. Box 200
Amarillo, TX 79168-0001
806-376-4811

American Youth Horse Council
4193 Iron Works Pike
Lexington, KY 40511-2742
800-TRY-AYHC

Appaloosa Horse Club, Inc.
P.O. Box 8403
Moscow, ID 83843-0903
208-882-5578

**Arabian Horse Registry
of America**
12000 Zuni Street
Westminster, CO 80234-2300
303-450-4748

Canadian Pony Club
National Office
6th Floor
1 Rideau Street
Ottawa KIN 8S7, Canada
613-241-7429

**CHA—The Association for
Horsemanship Safety and
Education**
5318 Old Bullard Road
Tyler, TX 75703
800-399-0138

Future Farmers of America
P.O. Box 15160
Alexandria, VA 22309
703-360-3600

National 4-H Council
7100 Connecticut Avenue
Chevy Chase, MD 20815-4999
301-961-2830

**North American Riding for the
Handicapped Association
(NARHA)**
P.O. Box 33150
Denver, CO 80233
800-369-RIDE (7433) or
303-452-1212

Pony of the Americas Club
5240 Elmwood Avenue
Indianapolis, IN 46203-5990
317-788-0107

The United States Pony Clubs
4071 Iron Works Pike
Lexington, KY 40511-8462
606-254-PONY (7669)

**Welsh Pony and Cob Society
of America**
P.O. Box 2977
Winchester, VA 22604-2977
703-667-6195

Acknowledgments

I would like to thank the following people and organizations for their help with this book:

Katherine and Susan Waldrop; Betsy Daniel and the students at James River Riding School, Richmond, Virginia; Rachel and Shayla Saltz; Celia Geotzl and Melinda Cohen; Samra Zelman and Rebecca Yount; Jenny and Michelle Smith; Jamie and Marlene Blackburn; Level Green Riding School, Powhatan, Virginia; Michelle Rudick; Hillary McMann; Mimi Chubb; Stefani Stutz; Katie Kopensky; Ashley Kohler; Julie Cecere and the students at Rancho Bernardo Riding School, San Diego; Aynsley Wilton; Megan Tubbs; Erin Keck; Erin King; Sarah Lepley; Allison Heim; Sonia Bennett; Heather King; Barrett Wright; and Richmond Saddlery.